MW01165340

The Happy Hustle

The Happy Hustle

Transform the Way You Work

Julie Ball

Copyright © 2017 *Sparkle Hustle Grow.* All rights reserved.

No part of this publication may be reproduced, distributed, or transmitted in any form or by any means, including photocopying, recording, or other electronic or mechanical methods, without the prior written permission of the publisher, except in the case of brief quotations embodied in critical reviews and certain other noncommercial uses permitted by copyright law.

Cover Design: Carmen Vermillion, VermillionCreativeAgency.com
Interior Design: Alexa Bigwarfe of Write.Publish.Sell
www.writepublishsell.co
Editing: Taylor Roatch

Published by Kat Biggie Press.

ISBN: 978-0-9994377-0-4
Library of Congress Control Number: 2017955339
First Edition: September 2017

10 9 8 7 6 5 4 3 2 1

Contents

Dedication

To my family, for always being my biggest fans!

Introduction
My Story

I'm Julie Ball, Founder of *Sparkle Hustle Grow*, a monthly subscription box for female entrepreneurs. I launched my first business in 2011 and quickly recognized that working for myself was my happy place.

One of my biggest inspirations is the female entrepreneur community.

Ladies, we're killing it!

I see social media posts every day from women who are leading their businesses and raising their families in ways that are authentic, generous, and helpful. I created *Sparkle Hustle Grow* to do the same.

I became a digital entrepreneur while we were expecting our daughter, McKenna, in 2011. I just couldn't imagine working in corporate America any longer. Fast-forward through six years of running my own website design & development firm, I wanted to get out from behind the screen so I started side-hustling in the product space.

I looked back at my expenses to see where I was spending my money. I purchased books, online courses, and lots of office supplies. Lots.

I decided to combine those items into one product, delivered monthly in a fun-to-open package. And who doesn't love getting mail?

And so...the Sparkle Hustle Grow subscription box was born!

The best part? I've been able to achieve my own business goals while supporting other female entrepreneurs on their journeys toward success.

Introduction

I like to call it the #BestBusinessExpenseEver for the female entrepreneur.

I am very intentional about the contents of the box and consider quality, availability, how it will be used, etc. It must be practical AND pretty. Each month, I work with vendors (small, medium, and large), distributors, makers, and course instructors to put together a mix of items with the goal in mind of helping you grow your business and delighting you with fun goodies!

MY 3 LEADING PRINCIPLES:

- The "Hustle" can be happy!
- Follow "The Golden Rule".
- Personal growth and business development go hand in hand.

For the rest of this book, we'll go over how YOU can use the above principles to find your way to productivity and happiness in both entrepreneurship and in the rest of your life.

We'll break the principles down a little more into practical chunks, with tips for how to address the issues many female entrepreneurs face throughout their journeys.

Sometimes, the steps you'll need to take to become successful might contradict what you expected to hear, but take it in stride and think about how you can apply each of the following lessons I've learned over the past several years.

I'm going to teach you how to hustle happy!

We rise by lifting others.

Chapter 1
Collaboration Over
Competition

~⟳~

One of the best parts about being an entrepreneur is that I have the luxury to collaborate rather than compete with my fellow boss ladies.

A little competition may not have ever hurt anyone, as the saying goes, but it definitely doesn't really help much, either, especially if you get too caught up in it.

COMPETITION ISN'T PRODUCTIVE. COLLABORATION IS.

The vast reach of social media means that everyone's opinion is right out there for all to see. Ignoring those prolific opinions has become something of an art form. The internet has really changed the way we interact; it makes people brave and frees them of many of the consequences of behaving like a jerk in person. It's more productive to build up our fellow humans than it is to tear them down, but unfortunately, such unbiased love and acceptance seems to be preached far more often than it's practiced. Mommy wars abound, and we see of people's lives only the positives they want us to see. We live with this competition day in and day out, and it's positively exhausting.

The good news here is you don't have to buy into this imposed competition. You don't have to play that game. Instead of competing, choose to collaborate. Opt out of the negative connotations of competing with your peers and instead buy into working together. It can reduce a lot of stress in your everyday life, and it may provide exponential rewards in business.

If you're a female entrepreneur like me, you probably see incredible women doing incredible things all around you. They were doing that before you were clued in, but tapping into your own potential helps you see it. It helps you understand just how impressive their feats are.

Every one of those remarkable women has special skills and a particular sparkle that they add to everything they do. They inject a little bit of their awesome into every piece of work they churn out. You've got something unique to offer, too!

Now, imagine that instead of seeing those incredible women as competition, you decided to work together and help each other out. Even entrepreneurs that are working in the same space as you have something special to offer, and you have something special to offer them.

Building up the people around you doesn't bring you down one bit, but competing with your peers just might. When you encourage and help women fighting for their dreams just like you're fighting for yours, they're likely to do the same. Not only that, the rewards of doing good by people are more far-reaching. It's a balm to the soul. Being an entrepreneur can oftentimes seem like a lonely endeavor, but working with other brilliant women can help eliminate feelings of isolation.

As nice as it is to have a little expert help every once in a while, *giving help* is good for more than your business. It makes you feel good about yourself, and that's just as productive long-term as whatever project you worked on together. It ties into to the need for self-development that I mentioned in the beginning of this book.

Remember this: giving makes us truly happy, winning only provides us with a superficial and short-lived high.

I 100% believe in collaboration over competition. Seems many of our subscribers feel the same. We see them collaborating every day in our private *Sparkle Hustle Grow* Facebook group. Read some of the stories they tell about their experience with collaborations.

Collaboration Over Competition

I had the opportunity to collaborate with Christy Wright the creator of Business Boutique. I attended one of her Business Boutique events shortly before launching my business. Three months after the launch of my business, she invited me to be a guest on her podcast to share my "Business Boutique success story." It was a very fun and exciting collaboration because not only did we get the chance to talk about Business Boutique (her creation) and how much it is helping women around the country, we also got to talk about my business. It was a win-win for both of us. I was able to represent for her audience a real life, true story of how following her plan works in business and in return, my business was able to gain a lot of exposure to her audience. Collaboration above competition is always a win in my book!

Jessica Principe
Founder, *All Girl Shave Club*

Collaboration is key to success. I have collaborated countless times and always end up with amazing results because two heads are better than one. Two audiences are better than one as well! One collaboration that stands out for me was with Damita McGhee. She and I met in a Facebook group, quickly got to know each other by talking in the comments, and ended up Skyping. From there we decided to be guest speakers in each other's Facebook groups. We each brought different knowledge, engaged with each other's audience, and have built a life-long friendship. We met in person at a conference only about four months after meeting online, and it was like we had known each other forever!

Carrie Sharpe
Communication Consultant and
Speaker at
He Says, She Says

I had the chance to collaborate with Julie for her March 2017 SHG box and it was a blast! We met via a Facebook group and I was just launching my course on Handlettering for Digital Design. I had over 60 of her current subscribers at the time sign up and take my course. The feedback I got was amazing and it helped grow my email list as well.

Lilah Higgins

Owner & Executive Designer,

The Higgins Creative

Make Your Passion Your Paycheck.

Chapter 2
Do What You Love & Love What You Do

*B*eing an entrepreneur can be hard. It takes a lot of passion, hard work, and unwavering dedication to your business to really be successful. Entrepreneurship takes a lot out of you on the best of days.

It's almost impossible to pour that much into your work if you don't love it.

If you're going to jump head first into a business venture, you may as well build something that makes you happy. There's absolutely no good reason to not do what you love when you have the power to create it and to change it.

As an entrepreneur, you hold the cards. You get to choose what you do and how you make your living. Even if you're already up and running, you can tweak your processes and offerings so that you have more opportunity to love what you do.

You can also choose to contract out the necessary parts of your business that you don't love. There's surely a talented fellow entrepreneur out there who is more than happy to do the work that makes you not-so-happy.

You might be asking how in the heck are you supposed to decide what to do. Here are just a few questions you can ask yourself to help you find your niche if you haven't found a perfect fit already:

- What do you love? What do you enjoy? What makes you happy? It doesn't need to seem particularly profitable from the get-go. You can build a business endeavor from the building blocks of your passion in life, but first you have to buy into the idea for just a second that you can make money doing something you love. It's a tough concept to swallow sometimes, but it's an important part of becoming a happy hustler!

- What are you good at? Find a way to use your existing skill-set combined with something you love to begin developing a successful, fulfilling idea.

- What do you still need to learn and what do you want to learn? Rarely does any previous career provide you with every skill you'll need as an entrepreneur, so there will likely be some knowledge gaps you'll need to address. It's important that you take into account what you want to learn, too. If you've chosen a niche you love, learning more about it won't (usually) be a chore. It will be something you enjoy.

I asked *Sparkle Hustle Grow* subscribers - How did you find your passion or your purpose when it comes to your business? Tell us about the moment that you just had to follow your heart and how that has changed your life.

In Summer 2016, I noticed that our city was having its first marathon EVER! I called the Race Director to volunteer. About two months later, he called to tell me that he was canceling the race. Without thinking, I decided I would take it on as Race Director. Before I knew it, I was earning sponsorships, filming commercials, and truly making a difference in my community. I fell totally in love with race directing, community action, and springing social change. In fact, things got so busy with the race that I ended up at a crossroads: Do I keep my full time corporate senior management job and give up the race, or do I quit making someone else rich and follow my dreams? The decision was simple: Goodbye, corporate America! I put in a two week notice and never looked back. This seemingly scary decision was a complete no brainer for me because I found what I was meant to do.

Courtney Poullas

Youngstown Marathon Race Director

~~~

Initially I wanted to join LuLaRoe and sell the clothes because I was obsessed. And if I, self-proclaimed don't-invite-me-to-your-direct-sales-parties-I-don't-want-any-part-of-that-scheme was into it, I knew something was different and special about the company. Then, I started getting compliments on the clothes I was wearing. I started feeling damn good about myself which doesn't always happen when you've been "the big girl" all your life. I had a new favorite skirt. This skirt is feminine, flowy, and flattering. I wore it to work one day and a colleague saw me in the office, but I didn't see her. The next day she emailed me just to tell me how beautiful she thought I looked that day. I started crying at my computer! When your clothes fit well and you are comfortable, you really are able to feel confident about yourself no matter how big or small you are. I want every woman to experience that feeling I got when I read that email. This is my passion, this is what drives me in this business. I love getting messages from our customers saying how great they feel! I love seeing their faces when they step out from a changing room with something I picked out for them that they would've never reached for and they see that they look fabulous!

Joy Cadiz

Joy of *LuLaRoe Faye & Joy*

I am a huge believer in that statement (Do what you love. Love what you do.)! I worked for 17 years at a large Fortune 500 corporation in various secretarial and human resource roles. My HR job was eliminated back in 2010 and the only position available was in Logistics. So, for a year and a half I sat behind a keyboard entering customer orders and moving freight around the world. I HATED it!! I had a "niggling" in my head for some time that I wanted to start my own photography business, but I was terrified and needed a push to do it. I had just gotten married around that time and my husband and I had a discussion and we decided that I should go for my dream - I didn't want to regret it 20 years down the road. So...I made the scariest decision of my life and quit my steady income, good benefit, financial stability job to start Stacey Lyn Boutique Photography, LLC. I was not a risk taker back then (I've gotten better at it through owning my own business), so I was literally throwing up the night before I resigned!! BEST DE-CISION I EVER MADE:) I have not looked back and my life is infinitely better because of taking that leap of faith. I LOVE being a business owner, and, even though I some-times struggle, get frustrated, and scared I KNOW that I will be successful because I am following my true passion.

Stacy Lyn Dominici
Owner - *Stacey Lyn Boutique Photography, LLC*

Find Your Tribe and Love Them Hard.

Chapter 3
Thriving in Community

When I tell people that I work from home, they immediately have a vision of coffee, yoga pants, and a messy bun. They also think it must be nice to have complete freedom and no annoying coworkers to deal with.

While that works for me some days, other days I really need my community. I thrive in community. But when I work from home, I sometimes feel like I'm working on an island. That's one of the big reasons why I started *Sparkle Hustle Grow*.

The reality of working from home is that it sometimes can get lonely working by myself all the time. I get distracted by things like housework and preparing dinner or let's face it, Netflix (I'm looking at you, #GirlBoss series!). Sometimes I feel unmotivated, especially when it's the third or fourth day in a row when I am just wearing yoga pants while I work. It doesn't give me the right mindset that I need to feel inspired.

One more reality is that when you work at home you never really leave work. In my current situation, my office is set up in the sunroom. While it's a beautiful, light filled room to do my work in, it also opens directly to the kitchen, dining room, and otherwise our living space. There is no door, no boundary. It's like I can see my work all the time and it's so easy to just walk over to the desk to check another email or publish another social post. I never put it down. And that's not healthy.

I'm pretty much an extrovert and very comfortable in social situations. But when I work at home, I have fewer opportunities to be a part of communities. My limited time during the day for work hours oftentimes makes me believe that I need to stay at home, put my head down, and hustle. But we all know what happens when we hustle all the time... We get burned out.

It's so important for me to be surrounded by people that lift me up, inspire me, who I can learn from. Motivational speaker Jim Rohn famously said that we are the average of the five people we spend the most time with...Well, that doesn't apply if you spend all your time alone in your home office. I wanted to create a community of other female entrepreneurs so we know that we're not in it alone. The community's common ground is that we are all business owners who want to constantly learn and implement new tactics to help grow our businesses...and have fun while doing it!

Here are a few things you can do today and every week to find yourself in community:

- Find your people. This is so key. I spent many

hours testing out business groups, meet-ups, and other networking events that just were not a good fit for me. It's OK to not go back to those if they don't feel like the right fit or that they won't help you grow. Find your people and love them hard.

- Meetup.com is a great place to find people with like-minded interests, goals, and activities. You can filter it by location, but also by your interests – both fun or for business.

- Join Facebook groups that are filled with your community. I am a part of several groups that are primarily female entrepreneurs, but I also participate in other groups such as one specifically for subscription box business owners and another one just for moms in my town. Trust me when I say that it's not good enough to just join the groups. You're not going to thrive and make the quality connections that you are craving by being stagnant in these groups. It's OK to be a stalker for a few days to get a feel for the group and determine if you think they're your people...but don't expect to get much out of the group (from a community point-of-view) if you don't make efforts to participate or contribute to the community. Ask questions, answer questions, give feedback when asked, just genuinely be a part of it without trying to sell. You will get so much value out of these groups if you just be yourself without pushing your product or service. There is a time and a place for promos or sales pitches, but it does not exist in the first 48 hours after you join a group. Seriously, chill.

- As you connect with all these women, you may think it's a challenge - that they are spread out all across the country, but I think that's part of the fun of it. Have you ever done a virtual coffee chat? While you may never meet in person, that doesn't mean you can't see them live on a video chat. You can use Skype, Facebook Messenger, or something like Zoom to do a video chat. When I first heard about these,

I was very nervous because video used to make me a little bit anxious. But after the first coffee chat I had with a new colleague, I was so inspired and uplifted. I was immediately hooked. I try to schedule at least 1 to 2 virtual video coffee chats per week just to stay in touch, to run ideas past a sounding board... You know, someone other than my husband, my best friends who aren't business owners, and my six-year-old. If video makes you nervous, simply do a quick phone call instead, but I really feel so much more connected when I do a video chat. If you want to learn more about Coffee Chats, I recommend the #SocialGlue Playbook by Reina Pomeroy at Reinaandco.com.

- Coffee chats are another great way to find an accountability partner. Maybe you schedule a coffee chat with the same person once a month as a virtual check in. Talk about goals, progress towards meeting those goals, and throw in a little bit of personal catch-up time just so you can build a deeper connection with them as a friend and colleague.

Here's what one of our subscribers said about finding her "tribe":

I am surrounded by hard working business owners who are equally just as hard working and amazing at being mamas. My business really started to thrive when I found "my people". Locally, I have a good core group of friends who also run super cool businesses and we try to get together as much as possible for coffee dates or play dates with our kids. Sometimes we bounce business ideas off each other but sometimes we just chat and know we can relate to each other's struggles and successes both professionally and personally. I always leave feeling energized and hopeful after any interaction with my tribe. Over the last year I've been fortunate to find my tribe online too in Facebook groups like *Boss Mom, She's Building her Empire*, and *Sparkle Hustle Grow*. Whenever I pop online I am blown away by the motivating women I get to be in the same groups with and it has help me push myself to grow as a business owner.

Renae Gonzalez
Owner, *Little Miss Everything*

The more you thank life,
the more life gives you to be
thankful for.

Chapter 4
Practicing Gratitude

Natalie Fox, author of *Gratitude Journal – 100 Days of Gratitude Will Change Your Life* – recently dropped some science bombs on me when I asked her about her gratitude journal.

Here's what she said: "When you are using it, you are actually exercising the neurons in your left pre-frontal cortex... The happy place! This takes you to a positive part of the brain where you can assess situations accurately and come up with excellent solutions to problems naturally. Here is where the magic happens and after a while you will start to see huge changes in your life! In fact, it doesn't really matter what you write, as long as it is positive because you bypass the parts of the brain that initiate the fear/flight/negative responses in your body and mind."

Start a gratitude journal. Write in it every single day; give yourself a little time every day to think about what you're grateful for and document it. Use your creativity and draw, color, and work up cute fonts so that it's aesthetically pleasing to you, as well. That extra touch of effort will make your gratitude journal a release in multiple ways.

Some days are just hard, and it's difficult to think of something you're grateful for in the now. That's okay! Instead, think of something from the past that you're grateful for. Take that memory and write it out in detail. Add drawings or color and open yourself up to the positive feelings you felt while making this memory.

If you can't come up with a happy memory, look

to the future for your positivity. The future holds boundless possibility. Think about how fantastic a future event will be. Push yourself to dig in and imagine the incredible positive changes your chosen event will have in your life. Now, write it all down! The here and now aren't necessarily the important part of this exercise. The point is that happiness attracts happiness, and you have the power to change that tide in your life. A gratitude journal is one very effective way to do that.

Worst case scenario - On days where I'm really down, I've even written the same thing over and over and over again. For instance: "I'm grateful for my amazing good health."

Stop for one second. Were you going to turn this exercise into something stressful? Find a way to blame yourself for not doing it well enough? Don't! Do your best and keep writing every day. If you're struggling, just make a run at journaling. Then, get a good night's sleep and let the stresses and anxieties of yesterday melt away a little. You'll probably find it a little easier when you're well rested. If nothing else, you can be grateful for good sleep!

Speaking of good sleep...Does your mind race at night? Not a surprise if you run a business! I like to pair up Kava Stress Relief Tea (by Yogi Tea) with my gratitude journal and a brain dump. A brain dump is simply when you write all your thoughts down on paper so your mind can rest. I find that this routine is a great way to end my day.

I try to actively **practice gratitude daily,** generally by writing it down in my Gratitude Journal. Putting your mind into a space of being thankful for what you learned, what happened today, and being positive about the future makes doing business, even on the tough days, an exciting experience. Need some ideas on how to practice gratitude in your life? Read on to see how some of our subscribers practice gratitude:

Each week, I make two lists: things that went right this week and things that went wrong. I evaluate both lists and look to see where I can make improvements. One of my biggest struggles is setting goals without planning out the action steps that I need to take to reach them. Keeping these two lists and working on them every week allows me to stay consistent with the actions that will allow me to reach my goals.

Melissa Cassidy

CEO - *Embrace Fit*

I practice gratitude by sending hand-written Thank You notes or special gifts given to clients.

Amanda Hollingsworth

Gratitude in business is so difficult because you feel like you need every resource you can get to grow your business and gain an advantage in your industry. It's so hard to be thankful when your bank account is running dry, your business isn't growing and it seems like everyone else is succeeding while you are failing. But by taking some of what you have, and intentionally and regularly giving it to others like children's organizations, your focus moves from yourself to others. And the impact of selfless and loving acts is amazing!!

Rachel Ingram

Author of *Joy & Finley,* *Barefoot Books Ambassador*

Be the reason someone else

smiles today.

Chapter 5
Making Others Happy through Amazing Customer Service

~

I take joy in amazing customer service. When I experience it, I feel good. When I practice it, I feel good.

My favorite thing to do is surprise someone with

the unexpected...like handwritten thank you notes or extra goodies in their packages!

Offering great customer service is good for business. That's obvious, right? People come back for more when you go above and beyond to take care of them.

As an entrepreneur who is likely taking on a lot of the face-to-face, day-to-day communications with clients or customers, you're the driving factor behind good customer service. It's your job and your job alone most of the time. While this can be a little stressful sometimes, it gives you an edge. You set the tone. It means that you have control over each customer service interaction. You alone have the power to make your clients happy, keep them coming back for more, and inspire recommendations to their peers.

How can you up your customer service game? Here are a few ways you can help each customer service contact go smoothly:

- **Listen**: If someone is contacting you with an issue, it's going to be a lot more productive

for everyone if you first simply listen and acknowledge a problem.

- **Fix it**: Take clear and decisive action to fix the
problem. Make sure you give the customer a
run-down of how you'll address their issue
in the simplest language possible. If a wide-
spread issue crops up, be honest about what's
going on with your customers, and take steps
to remedy it ASAP. I've found that transparen-
cy speaks volumes. So, own your mistakes if
needed!

- **Breathe, bless, release:** Sometimes people
get a little more aggressive with digital inter-
actions (as opposed to face-to-face) and tone
can be misinterpreted. If you are rolling your
eyes about a customer service interaction,
take a moment before you reply. My mantra:
Breathe, bless, and release. Then either respond to them with a more level head or ask
a friend or colleague to assist you with your
response.

- **Be expedient**: Apply fixes, respond to customers, and take feedback into account quickly. Of course, relegate these things to your office hours. You're not a machine!

- **See the value in every customer encounter:** Every time you speak with a customer or client, you have the opportunity to prove to them they made the right choice in using you. Take advantage of that constant flow of positive PR.

On top of being good for business, providing excellent customer service feels good. We've already established in the section on collaboration that doing right by people has direct positive effects on our mental state, not to mention the fact that it feeds our positive relationships with those around us.

Even when you're dealing with a person who isn't necessarily very pleasant or very grateful for your incredible and generous customer service, try to focus in on the fact that you're doing what's right for the customer and for your business. Remember that, even when people aren't acting very worthy of your extra effort. Each and every interaction reflects on your business. It makes it what it is in the eyes of your clients. Give them something positive to talk about.

We asked *Sparkle Hustle Grow* subscribers to share their stories about an amazing customer service experience! Here are two of our favorites:

Making people happy makes me happy so customer service is something that is very important to me. I love throwing in extra surprises for our customers to let them know how important they are to us. We recently had a customer who ordered a group order of tank tops for a bachelorette party she was going to. She had just had a baby a couple of weeks ago and she was organizing her friend's party and preparing to leave her newborn to attend the festivities. When I was a new mom I just so happened to do the same thing for one of my friends so knew exactly how she was feeling. I bundled up her order and threw in some things for her little Miss and a note and she was beyond grateful when she opened up the order and found the surprises for her and her new daughter. It's important to have a high standard of customer service and as often as possible try to set the standard a little higher for yourself because it makes you feel great when you make others feel great.

Renae Gonzalez
Owner, *Little Miss Everything*

Disney is the master of customer service. No one does customer service better. Each member of the Disney team is trained to treat their guests with respect, look them in the eye, and go above and beyond to ensure a good experience. My family has traveled to Disney World multiple times because of their attention to detail in making everyone feel special!

Carrie Sharpe

Communication Consultant and Speaker at *He Says, She Says*

Strive for progress, not perfection.

Chapter 6
Give Yourself a Break

*I*t's so important to give yourself a break when you are always hustlin'. Mistakes happen. We miss goals. I mean, nobody's perfect. Right? Give yourself some grace!

That's easier said than done sometimes, especially when we're talking falling short in our businesses. Generally speaking, there's a lot riding on our success, and oftentimes we're not the only people affected.

I'll almost guarantee that the people around you aren't nearly as disappointed in you about your imperfections as you are. Your partner likely won't think twice if you fall short of a goal. Your children are still going to think you're a total rock star regardless. Team members are probably not thinking about your failure so much as they are their own.

We truly are our own worst critics. So you've messed up. It happens. If it hasn't happened to you yet it probably will at some point. The first thing you'll need to do is take a short minute to mourn whatever loss this fail caused you. It's important that we open ourselves up to the way these things make us feel so that we can move on.

Progress over perfection.

Next, allow yourself to be human for a second. I mean, you are. We all are. As superhuman as being a rocking business lady can make us feel, we're still human. Just accept that you make mistakes and you're not perfect. It doesn't mean you're okay with mediocrity or failing, but it will allow you to rise above your mistakes.

If there's a way to make amends or an apology you need to give, go ahead and get that done. Even if it means eating a little crow or dropping a little cash to fix your mistake, I promise you'll feel better for it in the end. Let your heart be the driver of your business.

Now, you'll need to make a conscious step forward. There was a setback, but you'll pull yourself up, dust yourself off, and carry on. Don't let the negative define where you go from there. Resolve to do it better next time, take a second to learn from your mistake, and just keep going.

The good news is that ***you are not alone***. Nobody's perfect! Maybe you will relate to some of our subscribers' stories about a time when they fell short, made a mistake or just didn't feel good about their business.

This happened to me when I made the decision to push for the top level within my company's compensation plan. It was November of 2015 and I had made the announcement that my team and I were going for it. We all worked very hard and it came down to the last minute. We fell short of our $80,000 goal by $825! I felt completely defeated and embarrassed. It was a humbling experience and now is one of the juiciest parts of my story. We hit the top of the company three months later in February of 2016.

Tia Lukehart
Black Status Presenter with *Younique*

I JUST came out of a really tough week emotionally. I had lost several bookings and none were on the horizon. I was losing faith that anyone would EVER pay for my photography and was feeling like a failure. I literally eat, sleep, and breathe my business. It's my baby. The rejection can be extremely hard to take when a potential client chooses to go elsewhere or decides that they don't have money in their budget right now to make a purchase even though they LOVE their images. I tend to push, push, push - that's my nature. But... based on the advice of a great friend, I took a break! For almost a week, I just stopped. I filled my hours with things that bring me joy - singing, meditating, spending time with my loved ones, and a little bit of shopping;) It didn't happen immediately, but over the course of that week, I slowly began to climb out of my funk and was re-energized and ready to get back at it. Funny thing, too, once I climbed out of my funk several wonderful opportunities came my way, along with several inquiries. It's hard to remember when things aren't going your way, but being a business owner is a cyclical roller coaster ride of being "up" and "down". We just have to hold on tight and ride it out until we're back on top again!

Stacy Lyn Dominici
Owner - *Stacey Lyn Boutique Photography, LLC*

Ask yourself if what you are doing today is getting you closer to where you want to be tomorrow.

Chapter 7
It's Okay To Say No

I like to say yes. I like to overdeliver on my yes's. But sometimes, I just have to say no. Sometimes we say yes to too much...so much that we get spread thin and lose our true focus. We have to remember that it's okay to say no.

It isn't good for business for you to over-extend yourself. While it may seem that more must be better, that's not always the case.

The following are some considerations to help

you decide when saying yes may be detrimental to your heart, mind, and/or business.

You've got to make sure you leave room for your current clients or customers or orders. As an entrepreneur, you've always got obligations. You've got promises to fulfill. If saying yes may negatively impact your ability to meet your current obligations, your answer must be a resounding no, even if it's something that you'd really like to do. Instead, see if you can think of a way to fit the new endeavor in on your terms.

You also must make sure you're leaving room in your mind and your schedule to allow for the growth of your business in the direction of your choosing. You've got big plans for your business, right? You've set goals for the future. Consider whether saying yes will put you off track in achieving those goals before committing. Don't let a pop-up opportunity keep you from having room in your life for achieving your dreams.

Consider saying no to any task or project or client that doesn't make you feel properly valued. Even if once upon a time you were fine with the way things were working with a certain client in a particular branch of your business, the minute it stops feeling like it's worthy of your time and attention, begin planning your exit. There will always be someone or something that requires more than you can comfortably give, and even if you're already involved, give yourself permission to opt out. Obviously, you've got to remain professional in circumstances like that, but that doesn't mean you've got to be a pushover. Set your own boundaries, make well-thought out decisions, and proceed with grace.

This is another one of those times when you've got to exercise your rights as the keeper of your kingdom. Take full advantage of the fact that you have the power to choose where you extend your resources. You're good at what you do, and sometimes that means you may wind up with people trying to put more on your plate than you're comfortable with. Sometimes the problem will be that *they're* not willing or able to give as much as you need.

Avoid hard feelings when someone asks too much, just offer a polite, "No, but thank you for the offer," and carry on. If you don't want to or don't see the point in it, you don't need to explain yourself. Just say no.

I've "broken up" with clients in the past and politely declined projects because it just didn't feel like a good fit. One time in particular, it was a long-term client of several years, but our businesses were going in different directions and that's okay...It happens. You know what? As tough as the conversation might have been at the time, I always felt a huge weight lifted off my shoulders after I delivered my decision. By saying no to things that don't align with your goals, it opens doors to new opportunities.

I asked *Sparkle Hustle Grow* subscribers about a time when they had to say no and how it made them feel. Was it difficult? A relief? Did it open them up to new opportunities or maybe even allow them to focus more on what's important? Keep reading to see if you relate.

I fired my first client in the spring of 2017 and it was such a relief. We ended well, I was simply moving onto a different area of design, and an entirely new realm of pricing, and her projects no longer fit in my scope. I tell fellow designers often that it's okay to cut clients where you're not thriving. We're meant to thrive, and to do that, we have to learn to say "no."

Lilah Higgins
Owner & Executive Designer,
The Higgins Creative

I recently set business hours for myself. This was a huge change for the people pleaser in me. I wanted to respond to every order, every message, every text right away. Even if it meant I was up until 3 am on a "school night". I began to realize that this was cutting into time with my family, and time that I should have been using to take good care of myself. So, I set a certain time each day that would be used for business and business only. This has actually increased my productivity, and I've found a great balance.

Leah Wachna
Founder, *Sparkle Social*

I turned down a promotion at work. A leadership position. They immediately called me and asked me what they could do for me. I said, "It doesn't fit into my endgame right now." They gave me the raise anyway as well as assigned me to rewrite the job descriptions for the entire company. We are located in 13 states. Because I had the boldness to say no. But that took a process.

Charity Jones
Founder/Creator, *What's Your Endgame*

Little things can make a big difference.

Chapter 8
Make A Difference

As an entrepreneur, you have the power to give back and make a difference in this world more than the average person. Your reach is extended and your voice is just a little louder because of the position you've built for yourself.

Giving to those in need, whether it's time, money, or your remarkable entrepreneurial skillset, is valuable simply as an act of charity. It's the right thing to do good in the world. There's a little more behind my encouragement, though.

Giving back is one of the most intensive acts of self-care you can take on. People who help other people tend to be happier and more fulfilled. Doing good makes us feel good, and feeling good makes us better at our jobs. Aside from the personal value that we gain from making a difference, there are a ton of potential business benefits.

First, it's great PR for your business. It gets your name out there and it helps boost your reputation as a good person. People like to give their business to good people. Have you ever gone out of your way to spend your dollars at a company that's doing good for others? I'd guess the answer is "Yes".

Second, it's an awesome networking opportunity. Through your good deeds, you may have the opportunity to meet potentially beneficial contacts that you wouldn't have met otherwise. Their perspective of you will likely be favorable, as well.

Third, it may present you with the opportunity to learn new skills. People tend to be a little less picky about your particular credentials when you're donating your time to them, but the experience that you gain will resonate just as well or better than if you'd gained it in a traditional work environment.

Who wouldn't want to jump on an opportunity that's so fulfilling and valuable at the same time? Read this story about a *Sparkle Hustle Grow* subscribers making a true difference!

Moments that really make me feel like a champ are when people contact me because they see the work I do and they want me to share my story. At least a couple times a year I get contacted by our local Girl Scout leaders to talk to their Girl Scout troops about being a woman and running a business while running a family and it's the BEST. FEELING. EVER. I do what I do and lead the life I lead not to get recognition but to be a good role model for my daughters, but when other women want me to talk to THEIR daughters because they feel that I'm a good role model for them too I feel like a freaking rock star. I think times can be tough for all kids these days, especially girls, so I think it's so important to give them an environment where they can thrive, so I feel like I'm doing my job when people acknowledge that in some little way I'm doing that and want me to tell my story to the next generation so they can have a little insight on how to do that, too.

Renae Gonzalez
Owner, *Little Miss Everything*

Be good to yourself.

Chapter 9
Self-Care

*W*hen was the last time you took a break while you're working? Because I only have so much time to do my work each day – between 8 AM to 2:30 PM when my child is at school – I tend to try and cram in as much work as possible. I know that's not good for me. It's not good for my mind, my body, or my soul.

I find it hard to stop work when I get in my zone,

but taking a break can really rejuvenate you and get those creative juices going again. In order to make it the priority that it should be, I time-block breaks. I start my morning with a 30-minute cardio workout at the gym. I make sure to ink it in my planner so that it actually happens. I find if I write things in my planner rather than just think about them, then they actually become reality. There's something about taking the intention from my mind and writing it down in ink that makes it more concrete.

Throughout the day, I time-block break sessions. Some things that I like to do include simply stretching, going out on the porch or for a quick walk, taking a shower, yoga, meditation, or a coffee chat with a friend or colleague. Spending a few minutes on the phone or video chat with like-minded women can really change the trajectory of the day. I work from home by myself. Sometimes it feels like I'm on an island, so taking a break and making those connections is so crucial to my mindset and my happiness.

I've listed a few resources below that I personally use and recommend for these breaks, and I've asked my subscribers to chime in and let me know what they do for their breaks. How do they prioritize them? What do they do during their breaks? And how do they feel after they've given themselves a break? C'mon gals, you hustle hard all week. Don't you think you deserve a break? Darn right you do!

- Set an alarm on your phone or calendar for breaks – Plan them like you would plan a meeting.
- Yoga or Stretching – One of my favorites is Irena Miller. Irena's yoga creates bite-sized yoga videos for busy, intuitive, playful peeps on the go! http://www.irenamiller.com.
- Exercise – Even a quick walk can help you get refocused.
- A meditation app like Calm or Headspace.
- Treat yourself! A pedicure or a massage always does the job for me!

Burnout is real, and it's no fun at all!

So, we asked *Sparkle Hustle Grow* subscribers how they prevent it...

I have very specific work hours and I do my best not to work outside of those. All of my clients know my limits and have thus far respected them. My husband holds me accountable to my work time and helps me choose to be present when it's family time. This helps me avoid burnout because I'm practicing intention in all areas of my life, therefore no single thing is able to take over and create chaos in my life.

Lilah Higgins
Owner & Executive Designer, *The Higgins Creative*

I think it's so important to make time for things that recharge and relax you. For me, that's making time to exercise 3 times a week in the mornings before everyone else wakes up, going for walks in my neighborhood during lunch or taking the kids for a hike on the weekend. I also try to fit in a mani/pedi every couple of weeks as my splurge. I love my business, but I also recognize that making time for myself helps to refuel me so that I can give more to my business in the long run.

Jessica Principe
Founder, *All Girl Shave Club*

Burn out is the worst! I make myself take quiet time timeouts (normally three days in a row on those days' afternoons) and only allow for things I really wish I had more time for that never really get scheduled. Some of the things include an afternoon at an art gallery, book store to read magazines, read a book, paint or color, send hand written cards to people you care about etc... No TV, planner, phone, or computer time allowed.

Amanda Hollingsworth

You got this.

In Closing

A happy entrepreneur is a successful entrepreneur.

I'm guessing that you started your gig because you wanted a happier life. You wanted a path that you could pave yourself so that it fit better into your ideal world. Maybe you set out looking for grandeur, or maybe you just wanted to be there more often for the ones you love. Whatever your reasoning, the steps I've covered here can help you reach your goals with a happy heart.

The Happy Hustle

Those goals equate to more than the size of your bank account or the number of team members you've acquired. None of that really matters if you don't love what you do.

Make sure you put a little happy in your hustle.

Acknowledgements

When I first decided to write a book, I knew immediately that I couldn't do it on my own. Although I have a lot to say, putting it into perspective proved challenging. So I made a list of whom I'd ask for help and here's how that played out...

First, I joined a 30-day book writing challenge that my colleague, Liz Thompson of *House Style Editing*, hosted. This got me on track with my book concept, deadlines and motivated me to push forward. So thank you, Liz.

Next, I asked *Sparkle Hustle Grow* subscribers to be a part of it, of course! They are my people, my community and this book was my chance to give them a voice to share their stories. I was amazed at the overwhelming response and want to thank everyone that submitted a story!

After writing and collecting stories, I looked to the amazing Taylor Roatch to pull it all together in one linear, cohesive story. I tend to digress in my writing...go figure - what with 10 other tabs open on my laptop at the same time. So thank you, Taylor.

I wrote a book. Now what? I knew exactly whom to ask: Alexa Bigwarfe of *Write.Publish.Sell.* I met her (and virtually half of everyone else involved) through the *Boss Mom* group. She took my manuscript and literally breathed life into it. A big thank you to Alexa and to the *Boss Mom* group.

Thank you to Carmen Vermillion of *Vermillion Design*, my dear friend and the brilliant designer behind the *Sparkle Hustle Grow* brand and the cover art on this book. With my design projects, you have the incredible ability to get it right *on the first try* almost every single time!

Thank you to *Becca Bond Photography*, who has documented virtually my entire adult life – both

Acknowledgements

personal and business – and became a very close friend along the way.

I also want to acknowledge my friend, colleague, and subscription box bestie, Jessica Principe – Founder of *All Girl Shave Club*. You inspire me and challenge me to make good business decisions. You are a rock star.

Thank you deeply to my husband, Kenny, and our daughter, McKenna, for standing by my side through yet another work project. Thank you for giving me the time, space and love needed to complete it.

Thank you to my entire family, but especially my parents for always believing that I could be whatever I wanted to be, even if that sometimes was a gray area. Thank you for your encouragement, for packing up SHG boxes and for investing time, love and money into my crazy ideas.

And, an extra sparkly thank you to my closest friends and sources of support - Lisa, Jen, Brandi, Nathalie, Paisley, Melissa, and Meagan.

Throwing gratitude around like confetti!

Julie

About the Author
Julie Ball

After running a successful website design & development firm (Grow Web Marketing), Julie wanted to get out from behind the screen. This desire coupled with her biggest inspiration, the female entrepreneur community, is what led her to start *Sparkle Hustle Grow* (http://sparklehustlegrow.com), a monthly subscription box for female entrepreneurs.

Taking her knowledge of the entrepreneurial world and key products that had helped her grow her business, she combined them into one product, delivered monthly in a fun-to-open package and has been able to help fellow female entrepreneurs on their journeys toward success.

Although a Pittsburgh area native, Julie now lives in Black Mountain, an idyllic mountain town in Western North Carolina, with her daughter McKenna and husband Kenny. You'll find them hiking the local trails, listening to live music and otherwise enjoying mountain life with friends & family.